Neighborhood Birding 101

An Identification Guide to
Washington, Oregon & Northern California's
Most Common Neighborhood Birds

Seymore Gulls

Seymore Gulls

Seymore Gulls Field Guides
Portland, Oregon
seymoregulls.com

Photo Credits and Copyright information appear on page 159

Published in 2021 by Seymore Gulls
8910 NE Thompson St
Portland, Oregon 97220
seymoregulls.com

Library of Congress Cataloging-in-Publication Data

Gulls, Seymore, 1984 - , author.
Title: Neighborhood Birding 101: An Identification Guide to Washington, Oregon, and Northern California's Most Common Neighborhood Birds/ Seymore Gulls
Series: Seymore Gulls Field Guides | Includes Index.
Identifiers: LCCN 2021910795 (print)
ISBN 978-1-7371698-0-2 | ISBN 978-1-7371698-1-9 (ebook)
1. Birds - West Coast 2. Birds - West Coast - Identification 3. Bird Watching - West Coast

Book design and formatting by Eric R. Carlson

Printed in USA

10 9 8 7 6 5 4 3 2 1

Contents

Wetland Birds

1 Geese & Ducks
29 Shorebirds & Wading Birds
40 Swifts, Swallows & Hummingbirds

Birds of Prey

51 Vultures, Hawks & Eagles
73 Owls
76 Falcons

Forest Birds

79 Woodpeckers
85 Corvids
91 Chickadees, Kinglets, Nuthatches & Wrens

Neighborhood Birds

104 Pigeons & Doves
108 Thrushes
113 Finches
124 Sparrows
135 Blackbirds

Neotropical Migrants & Friends

142 Flycatchers & Warblers
155 Tanagers & Grosbeaks

159 Photo Credits & Copyright Information
162 Index

Cackling Goose
Small bill & steep forehead
Short neck
Gray body
White
Adorably small
Forms large winter flocks

Canada Goose
Big bill w/ gradual slope
White cheek & chin
Long neck
Big butt
BIG
White undertail
(Cackling Geese)
Loves fields

Mallard ♂

Green head

Yellow bill

White ring

Dark chest

Standard pond duck

Mallard ♀
Dark eyeline
w/ light eyebrow
Dark splotch
on orange bill
Mottled brown
plumage
Our largest dabbling duck

Northern Shoveler ♂

Winter wetland dabbler

Forms large spiraling rafts

Coarse streaks on head

Enormous shovel bill is distinctive

Gadwall ♂

Says "Hey. Hey. Hey."

Steep forehead

White secondaries

Black butt

Intricate mosaic pattern

 Gregarious wetland dabbler

Gadwall ♀

Dabblers feed in the shallows, face submerged, butt up

Peaked forehead

Thin bill edged in orange

White speculum

Light/white tummy

Found in pairs with males all winter

American Wigeon ♂

Makes kazoo whistling sounds

American Wigeon ♀

Brown/gray head

Black tip

Dark smudge around eye

Rusty sides contrast w/ head

Enjoys a pond or grassy field

Northern Pintail ♂
Brown head
Pintail!
White neck stripe
Black butt
White breast
Found in large grassy wetlands

Northern Pintail ♀

Plain tan head

Dark mottled back

Long tail

Light buffy belly

Swims w/ chest low in water

Nervous dabbler

Green-winged Teal ♂

Cinnamon head w/ green streak

Green wing!

Buffy tail w/ black border

*Vertical white stripe is distinctive

Our smallest dabbler

Green-winged Teal ♀

Ring-necked Duck ♂

Black back

White outline on bill

Gray sides

↑ Bright white shoulder

 More like ring-billed duck, amirite?

Ring-necked Duck ♀
Peaked head
Ring!
White eyering
Creamy color behind bill
White line
Light-colored "spur"
Shy diving duck

Wood Duck ♂
Unmistakeable dream duck
Beautiful flowing rainbow
Stunning to behold

Wood Duck ♀

Nests & perches in trees

White around eye

Small bill

Blue & white speculum

Prefers densely wooded ponds

Bufflehead ♂

Iridescent black & white head

White chest & flanks

Pocket-sized diving duck

Bufflehead ♀

Black head w/
white dot
behind eye
(distinctive)

Small
bill

Little & gray

Adorable

Hooded Merganser ♂

Big head!

Often pops up long tail

Thin bill

Rusty sides

Black & white "hood" can be raised and lowered

Slim diver

Hooded Merganser ♀
Lowered
Frosted tips
Raised
Adjustable crest
Red eye
Gray-brown
Prefers forested wetlands

Common Merganser ♂

Dark, greenish head

Red "saw-bill"

White secondaries

White chest & sides

Swims w/ submerged butt

 Long-bodied freshwater diver

Common Merganser ♀

Chestnutty head

Shaggy crest

Crisp division of color →

White ↓

White chest

Gray body

Found on rivers and lakes

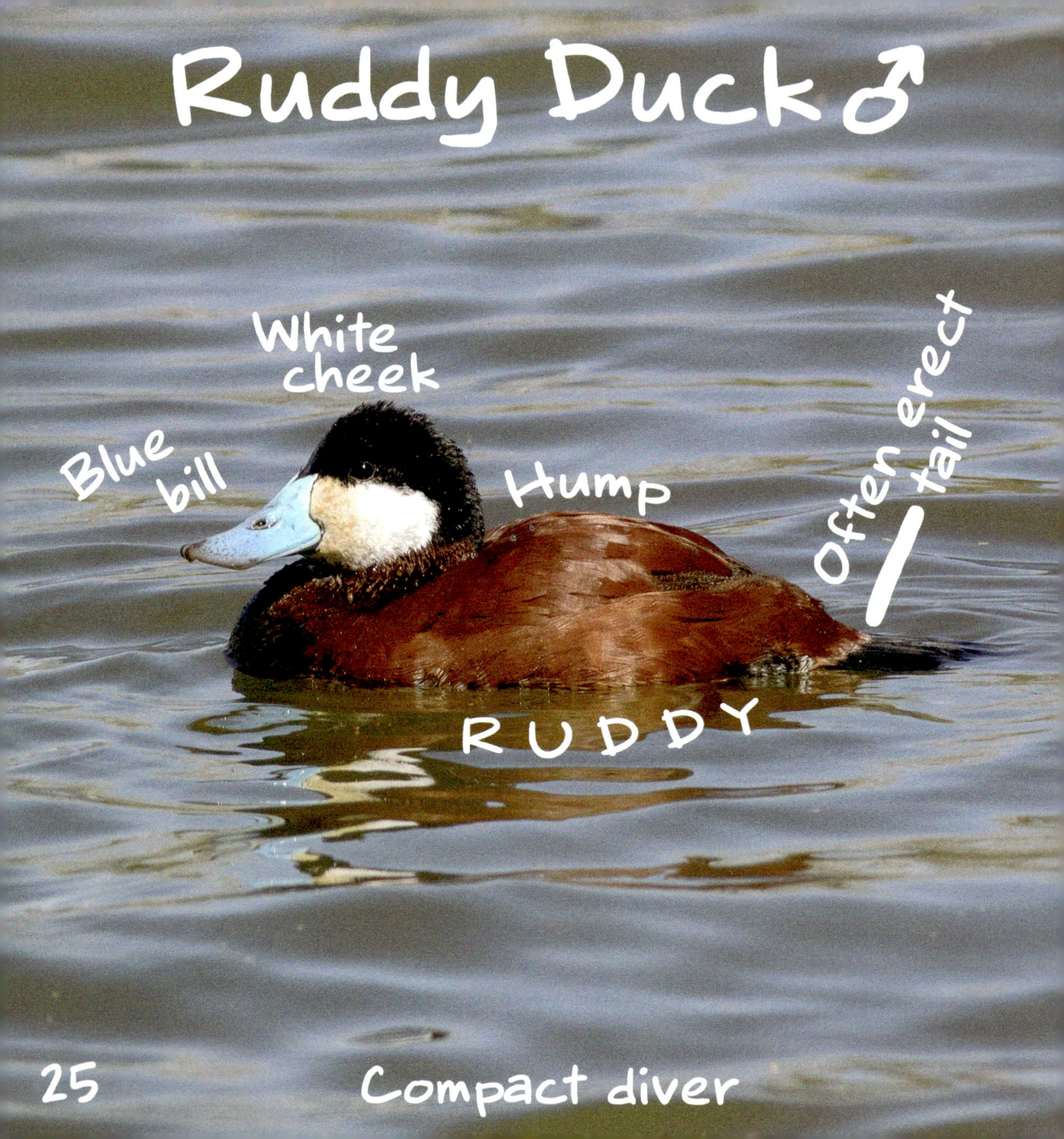

Ruddy Duck ♂

White cheek

Blue bill

Hump

Often erect tail

RUDDY

Compact diver

Ruddy Duck ♀
Dark cap
Dusky horizontal cheek stripe
Dark gray bill
Brown-gray
Likes open water w/ lots of vegetation
Forms large, homogeneous flocks

Pied-billed Grebe

Almost no tail

Black ring on pale bill

Small loaf of bird

Solitary diver

American Coot

White bill

Plump body

Uniformly dark gray

Large lobed feet

Omnivorous pond chicken

Killdeer

"Kill-DEER!"

Orange eyering

Stripy face

Two breast bands

White tummy

Year-round field/wetland parking lot plover

Greater Yellowlegs

Bill longer than head

Light speckles

Slightly upturned

Yellow!

"Deew deew deew"

Noisy and active shorebird

Spotted Sandpiper

(breeding adult)

Tail-bobbing brisk walker

Spotted Sandpiper

(juvenile/nonbreeding)

Crouched posture

Lightly marked tan back

Thin curved bill

No spots...

Drab yellow legs

Shorebird that likes dry feet

Great Blue Heron
Angry dinosaur sounds
HUGE!
Long tucked-in neck
Wispy feathers
Long legs
Not a crane

Great Egret

Yellow bill

Long S-curved neck

All white

Plumes

Black legs & feet

Patient hunter

Black-crowned Night-Heron
(adult)

Black-crown

Black back

White front

Squat & chunky

Short legs

Day roosting tree penguins

Black-crowned Night-Heron
(juvenile)

White spotting

"WOK!"

Yellowish bill

Streaky sides

Mostly nocturnal

Double-crested Cormorant

Green eye

Orange face

Often seen drying feathers (not waterproof)

Long neck

Long tail

Swims & perches w/ head tilted up

 Big black waterbird

Belted Kingfisher

Messy crest

Dagger bill

White collar

Dark band

No rufous belly band on males

Perches conspicuously above water

Plummets like a dart to catch fish

Black Phoebe

Hawks for insects

"fee-bee!"

Black top half

White bottom half

Lots of tail bobbing

Wetland flycatcher

Vaux's Swift

High-pitched twittering chips

During fall thousands will roost together in chimneys

High flying insectivore

Purple Martin

(male)

Techno-sounding calls

Peaked head

Nest in woodpecker holes and manmade bird condos

All blue-black

The big purple one

Purple Martin
(female/juvenile)

Large, long wings

Light collar

Light forehead

Dark back

Whitish belly

Our largest swallow

Tree Swallow

Black eye-mask

Metallic blue-green

White stops BELOW eye

Loves fields & wetlands

Violet-green Swallow

White on cheek goes ABOVE eye

Green back

White sides on rump →

Long wings

Quick & erratic aerialist

Barn Swallow

Blue cap & back

Rusty forehead & throat

Orange tummy

Pointy wings

Long forked tail

Classic bird tattoo

Cliff Swallow

Blue cap

Tan headlight→

Mud nests

Rusty beard

Dark back

Buffy rump

Colonial nester

Anna's Hummingbird
(adult male)

Anna's Hummingbird
(female/juvenile)

Straight bill

Dark spot →

Green back

Eats insects

Uses spider silk for nests

Plump

Common neighborhood hummer

Rufous Hummingbird
(adult male)

Winters in Mexico
Here: Mar-Sep

Buzzy wings
in flight

White chest

Coppery
gorget

Fiery!

Rufous Hummingbird

(female/juvenile)

Aggressive flower defender

Turkey Vulture

Soars w/ wings in shallow "V"

Tiny naked head

Often soars w/ multiple friends

Dark body

Light flight feathers

Loves roadkill

Osprey

Feet-first diver

Cooper's Hawk

(adult)

Dark cap

Stern look

Light nape

Eye closer to beak than nape

Steely blue back

Dense orange barring

Crow-sized yard predator

Cooper's Hawk

(immature)

Large, square head

Raisable hackles

Narrow streaks on pale front

Targets starling & robin-sized birds

White undertail coverts

White band on tip of long, rounded tail

Long hawk

Cooper's Hawk

(adult)

"t" shape in flight

Head sticks out past wings

Neck

Long tail

Orangish underside

Glides w/ slow, countable wingbeats

Sharp-shinned Hawk (adult)

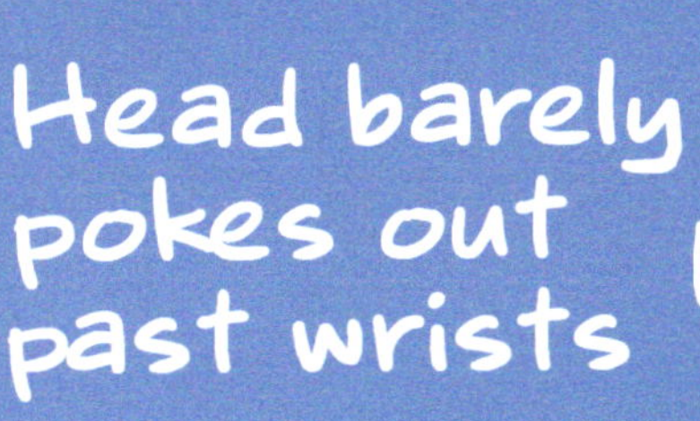

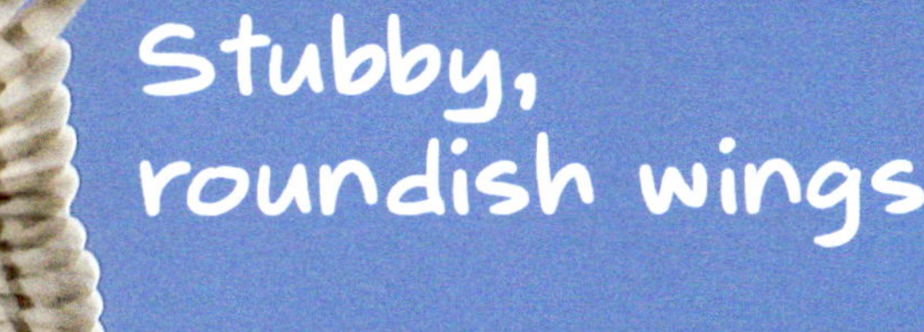

No neck

Shorter, boxy tail

Quick wingbeats in straight flight

Sharp-shinned Hawk

(adult)

Dark cap extends down the nape

Small, round head

No neck

Flicker-sized

Preys on sparrow-sized birds

Square tail w/ little to no white tip

Little accipiter

Sharp-shinned Hawk
(juvenile)

"Bug" eyed

Round head w/ no neck

Heavily streaked chest

Barrel chested

Skinny legs

Deep forest breeder

Bald Eagle

(adult)

White head

MASSIVE bill

Dark body

White tail

Big talons

Our national symbol

Bald Eagle
(immature)

Fish-eating eagle

Golden Eagle
(adult)

Golden Eagle
(immature)

Just 3 white patches

White flight feathers

Mostly brown

White base of tail

Dark tip

Rare:
N. of Medford, OR
or W. of Cascades

Red-tailed Hawk
(adult)

Ubiquitous hawk

Red-tailed Hawk
(juvenile)

Dark leading edge

Dark belly band

Uh-oh!

Pale-colored section

Variations on a theme

Red-tailed Hawk
(juveniles)

Two-toned wings

Often seen kiting & soaring

Red-tailed Hawk

(dark-morph adult)

20% of Red-tails are darker/lighter morphs

Pale spot

Does voiceovers for eagles on TV

Wide, short red tail

Screams: "keeeeaar"

When in doubt, its probably a red-tail

Red-tailed Hawk
(juvenile)

Standard color pattern:

Dark

Light

Dark

Large dark head

Light chest

Dark streaked belly band

This pattern describes approx. 80% of Red-tailed hawks

Roadside rodent hunter
(but not usually in the road)

Red-tailed Hawk

(juvenile)

Big head

Light feathers make a speckled "V" pattern on the back

Broad shoulders

Dark tail

Perches near open areas

Red-Shouldered Hawk
(adult)

Coarsly patterened back

Reddish shoulder

Rusty front

Thin light bands on dark tail

Bold black & white pattern

Wet woodland hawk

Red-Shouldered Hawk
(immature)
Plain head
Bit of rufous on neck/shoulder
Small bill
Coarsely patterend back
Medium-large
Banded tail
Hunts from forest-edge perches

Red-Shouldered Hawk

(adult)

Light crescents in primaries →

Black & white wings

Plain head

Banded tail

Reddish coverts →

Fine barring on tummy

Noisy jay-like calls

White-tailed Kite

Hovers high while hunting

Great Horned Owl
Ear tufts
Big eyes
Camouflage
Dense horizontal barring
73 Red-tailed Hawk of the night

Dark eyes

Round head

"Who cooks for you?!"

Scruffy neck

Light belly w/ dark streaks

Eats: birds, bugs rodents, crayfish etc...

Likes big trees

Barn Owl

Heart-shaped face

White speckled front

Shadowy blue & sandy wings & back

Similar habitat to kestrel

Really do live in barns

Night screamer

American Kestrel

Our smallest falcon

Sideburn

Mustache

Rufous back

Steely wings

Bespeckled

Murder parrot

AREA CLOSED

Winter falcon

Peregrine Falcon
(immature)
Dark hood
White cheeks
& throat
Barred
chest
Wide
shoulders
Pointy wings
Long tail
The fastest animal in the world

Downy Woodpecker

Bill half length of head

Red dot found only on males

"Pik!"

Black sides & tail

2" smaller than Hairy

Likes small branches

 Tiny neighborhood woodpecker

Hairy Woodpecker

Bill same length as head

"Speak!"

White tummy

White back

Found on trunks & large branches

Mature-forest woodpecker

Northern Flicker

 Common neighborhood drummer

Red-breasted Sapsucker

White dot

Red head & breast

Black back

White speckling

Gray barred flanks

Sap-well driller

Acorn Woodpecker

Red cap

Clown face

Makes thousands of small holes in dead trees to store acorns

Black chest & back

Streaks

White tummy

Oak forest clown

Pileated Woodpecker

Chisel

Red crest

HUGE!
(crow-sized)

Black body

Male: red mustache

Mature-forest resident

Our largest woodpecker

Steller's Jay

Dark crest

Dark head & back

Bright blue wings & tail

Blue belly

Bold & noisy

Coniferous forest jay

California Scrub-Jay

It's not a Blue Jay!

American Crow

"Caw! Caw!"

Slim, straight bill

Crow-sized

Smooth throat feathers

Loves unsalted peanuts

Neighborhood corvid

American Crow

Forms large winter gangs

Common Raven

Thick, curved bill

Shaggy
neck
beard

"Groak, Groak!"

Twice the size
of a crow

Solitary forest omnivore

Common Raven

Soars & does aerobatics

Our largest songbird

Black-capped Chickadee

Black cap

White cheek

Black chin

Gray back

Moves in mixed winter flocks

Attract w/ sunflower seeds

 "Chickadeeee dee deee deee..."

Chestnut-backed Chickadee
Chickadee head
Chestnut back
Evergreen & oak forest resident
Chestnut sides
West Coast chickadee

Oak Titmouse

Repetitive two-note songs

Adjustable crest

Range: S. OR & CA

Gray back

Stubby bill

Lighter gray tummy

 Oak forests & bird feeders

Golden-crowned Kinglet

Gold & black crown

Striped face

Yellowish back

Tiny bill

Mixed-flock chickadee friend

High-canopy conifer kinglet

Ruby-crowned Kinglet

Convertible ruby crown

Dark spot beside wing bar

Thin bill

Crisp yellow on black

Yellow feet

 Hyperactive shrub forager

Hutton's Vireo

Smudgy, light lores

Big head

Thick, grayish bill

Matte sheen to drab wings

Dark feet

Methodical branch hopper

Red-breasted Nuthatch

Female's belly is lighter red than male's

Conifer excavator

White-breasted Nuthatch
Attracted to sunflower seed feeders
Dark crown stripe
Chisel
White face & tummy
Deciduous forest descender
98

Bushtit

Loves suet & aphids

Hunts in packs

Round

Long tail

Little bill

Tiny!

Dark eye = male
Light eye = female

When not breeding:
in groups from 5-37

Brown Creeper

White unders

Light eyebrow

Creeps!

Flies to base of tree & creeps upward searching for food

Brown speckled back

Sings: "Trees, trees beautiful trees"

Active trunk ascender

Pacific Wren

Loud, complex song

Mousy color
Mousy size
Mousy lifestyle

Tail: popped

Barred wings & sides

Denizen of the forest floor

Bewick's Wren

Thin eyebrow

Brown upperparts

Barred tail

Light underparts

Our most common yard wren

Marsh Wren

Heard more often than seen

Dark crown

Light eyebrow

Dark back

Light throat & chest

Stiff tail

Hides among reeds & cattails

Spry wetland singer

Rock Pigeon

Iridescent nape

Majestic urban mascot

Band-tailed Pigeon

Perches high atop trees

White collar

Iridescent collar

Yellow bill

Loud clapping on takeoff

Pale gray & lavender

Band

Migratory forest pigeon

Eurasian Collared-Dove

Daytime hooting

Dark collar

Pale overall w/ dark primaries

Upright percher

Short tail

Chunky

Devours millet & grains

Mourning Dove
Blue eyering
Daytime owl sounds
Thin bill
Black spots
Long pointy tail
Slender
Red feet
107 Neighborhood & grassland dove

Western Bluebird

Attract w/ nest boxes
& mealworms

Blue head
& wings

Rusty
shoulders
& breast

Female paler
than male

Fields + trees = bluebird habitat

Hermit Thrush

Narrow,
white eyering

Gray-brown
back

Rusty
wing-edge

White
breast
w/ BOLD
spots

Rusty tail

 Furtive forest-floor forager

Swainson's Thrush

Buffy lores & spectacles

Migrates here to breed: May-Sep

Brown back & tail w/ little contrast

Grayish white w/ dark spots

"Pwip" water drop call

Flutelike summer singer

Varied Thrush

Spooky buzzy whistle

Male darker than female

Pumpkin eyebrow

Pumpkin throat

Breastband

Dark back

Scalloped tummy

Winter lowland visitor

American Robin

White face patterning

Yellow bill

Dark head & back

Orange tummy

Our most common thrush

House Sparrow

(male)

Gray crown

Rufous nape

Black lores

White cheek

Black throat

Noisy

113 Old world sparrow of parking lots

House Sparrow
(female)

Light eyebrow

Pale bill

Striped back

Gray-brown underparts

Competes w/ natives for nest boxes

House Finch
(male)

Brightest on forehead

Curved culmen

Pale cheek

Plumage ranges from yellow to red

Streaked sides

Ubiquitous feeder finch

House Finch

(female/immature)

Plain cheek & face

Long, blurry brown streaking

Long tail

Forms large, sunflower seed-eating flocks

Purple Finch
(male)

Red forehead & cheek

Light eyebrow

More raspberry less orange

Clean, unstreaked look

White belly

 In spring warbles from treetops

Purple Finch

(female/immature)

Lesser Goldfinch

(male)

White wing patches visible in flight

Black cap

Greenish back

Dark bill

Dull wingbars

White spot

Flocking thistle eaters

Lesser Goldfinch

(female/immature)

Drab green back

White spot

Pointy bill

Short tail

Clean, yellowish front

Our smallest finch

American Goldfinch

(male/breeding)

Black forehead

Flight call: "po-ta-to chip"

Orange bill

Yellow back

Black wings w/ white bars

Yellow!

 Attract w/ sunflower & thistle

American Goldfinch

(female/immature)

Conical bill

Yellow-brown back

Black wings w/ pale wingbars

Unstreaked, whitish tummy

Loves an unmown yard

Pine Siskin

Call:
"rising zipper"
Streaky back
Pointy bill
Yellow in wings & tail
Streaky front
Irruptive nomadic finch

Dark-eyed Junco

Dark hood

Pale pink bill

Brownish sides

White outer tail feathers

White belly

Joins winter sparrow flocks

Song Sparrow

Probably in your yard right now

Stripy gray & brown face

Stripy chest converges to dark spot →

△ ← Dark triangle

Long tail

Gray tummy

 Musical neighborhood sparrow

Fox Sparrow

Rounded head

Uniformly sooty head & back

Gray & yellow bill

Chunky brown triangular spots

Secretive ground-scratcher

White-crowned Sparrow (adult)

Crisp black & white crown

Black eyeline

Yellow-orange bill

Light brown back

Gray cheeks & tummy

 Year-round crowned sparrow

White-crowned Sparrow (immature)

Brown crown stripes

Dark eyeline

Yellow-orange bill

Long tail

Unmarked breast

Found in neighborhoods & clearcuts

Golden-crowned Sparrow

Thick, black eyebrow

Yellow forehead

Gray cheek

Gray bill

Plain underside

Gregarious: forms large winter flocks

Golden-crowned Sparrow

(immature)

Yellow forehead

Big for a sparrow

← Dark lores

Darker back

Plain unders

Winter sparrow

Migrates to Alaska in spring

White-throated Sparrow

Dark & tan crown stripes

Yellow lores

White throat

Smudgy chest

Light belly

Uncommon "crowned" sparrow

Spotted Towhee

Red eye

Black head & back

White ←spots

White tummy

Rufous sides

Big
(for a sparrow)

Long tail

Ground-scratching thicket skulker

Savannah Sparrow

Grassland songbird

Lincoln's Sparrow

Red-winged Blackbird ♂

Found in wetlands

Red & yellow shoulder patches

Black body

 Sings loudly from tops of cattails

Red-winged Blackbird ♀

Reddish tinge around pointy bill

Light eyebrow

Rufous edges on feathers

Dense streaking

Winner of the Most Misidentified Bird award!

Will come to bird feeders

Brown-headed Cowbird ♂

 Joins big mixed blackbird flocks

Brown-headed Cowbird ♀

Plain, brown head

Short pointy bill w/ thick base

Pale throat

Uniform dark body

Brood parasite:
lays eggs in other birds' nests

Brewer's Blackbird ♂

Forages in flocks

Brewer's Blackbird ♀

Our native parking lot bird

European Starling

Chin-up posture

Yellow bill

Mimics other bird calls

Shaggy throat feathers

Triangle spots

Iridescent purple & green

Short tail

Flocks in murmurations

Cedar Waxwing

Black mask

Mullet

Silky browns & yellows

Waxy wingtips

Eats berries & bugs

Olive-sided Flycatcher

Peaked head

Chunky triangle bill

White throat

Gray "vest"

Yellow tummy

Conspicuous perches

Short tail

 Says "Quick! Three beers!"

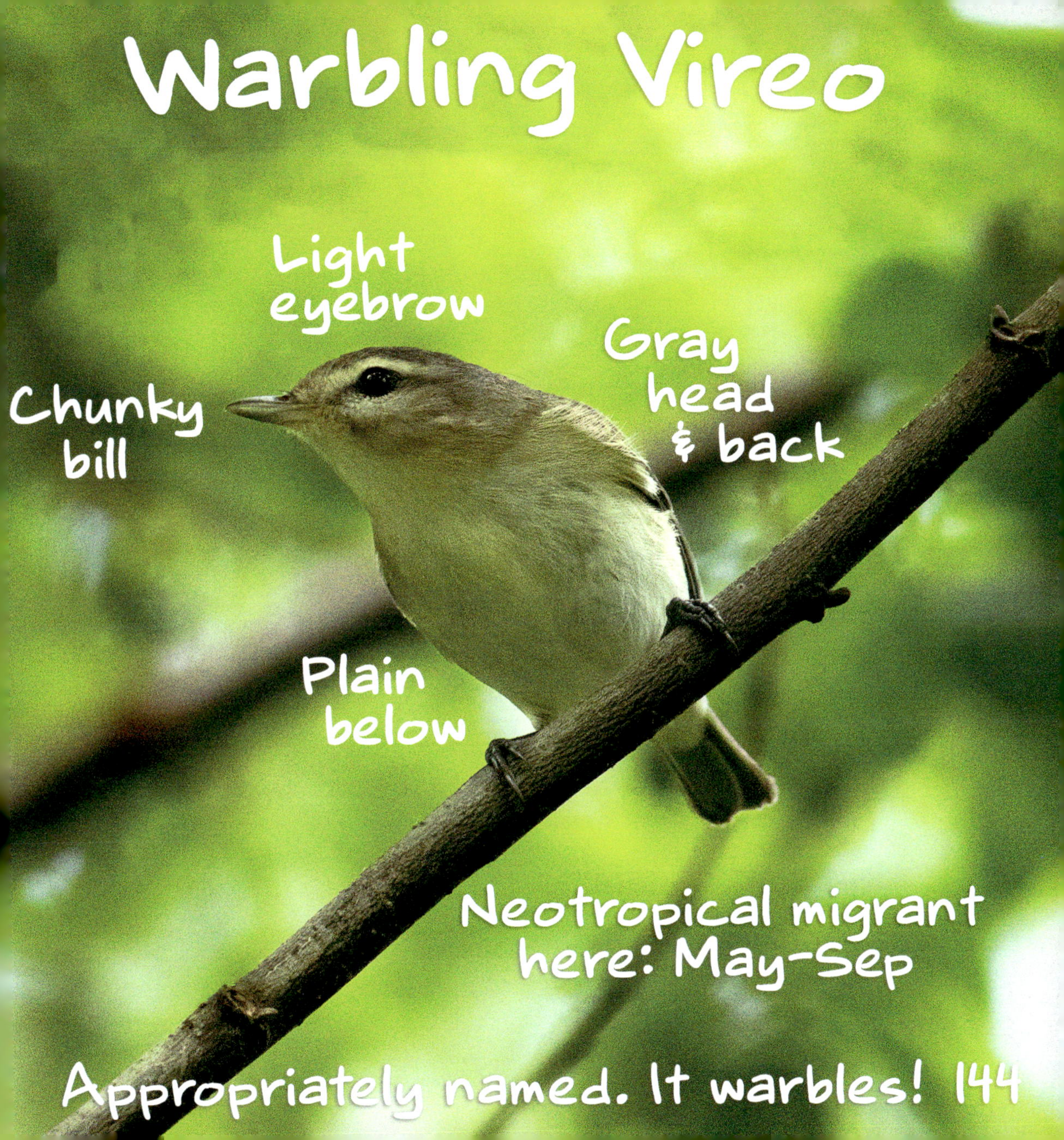

Warbling Vireo

Light eyebrow

Gray head & back

Chunky bill

Plain below

Neotropical migrant here: May-Sep

Appropriately named. It warbles!

Orange-crowned Warbler

145 Earliest migrating wood warbler

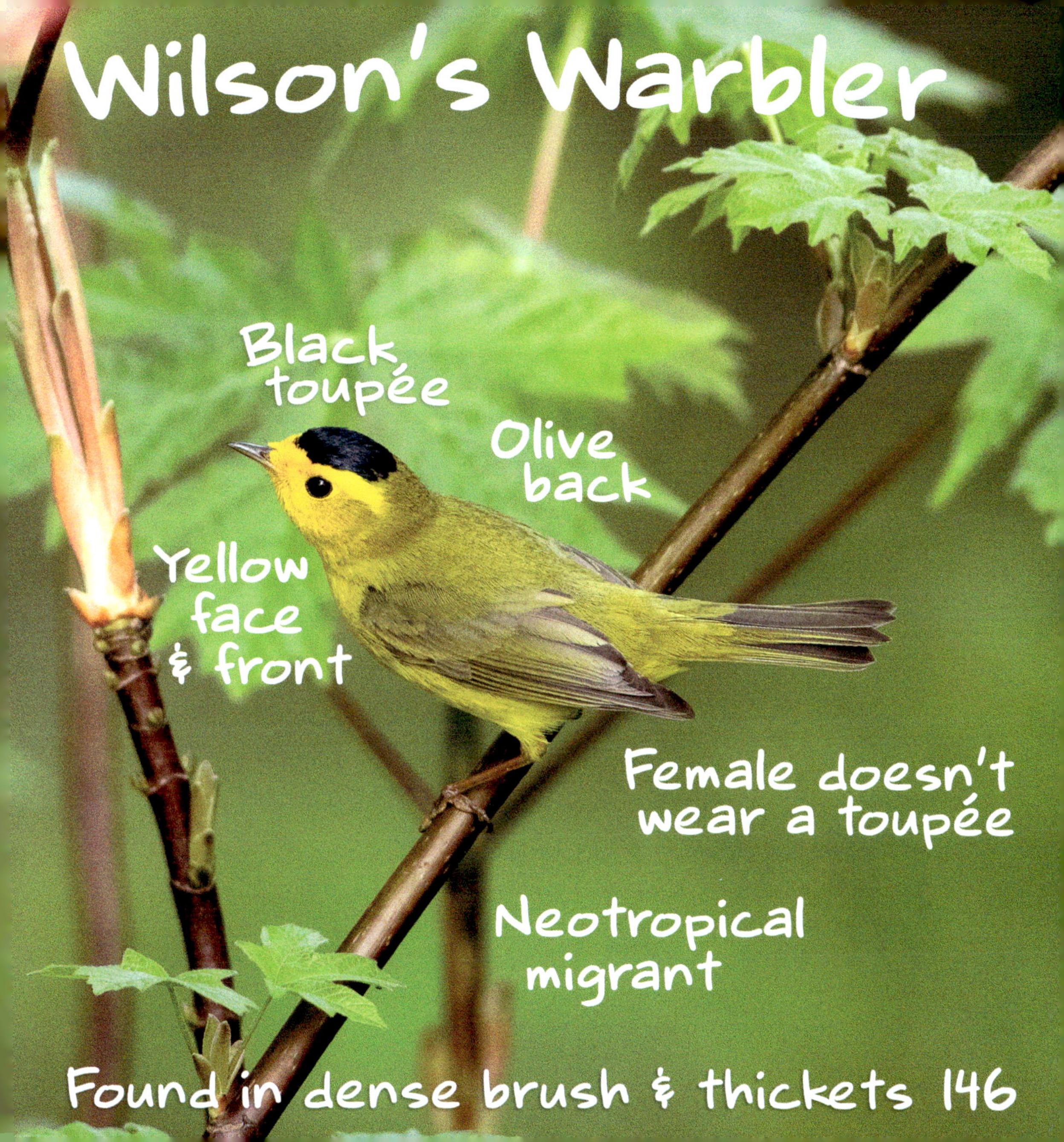

Wilson's Warbler

Black toupée

Olive back

Yellow face & front

Female doesn't wear a toupée

Neotropical migrant

Found in dense brush & thickets

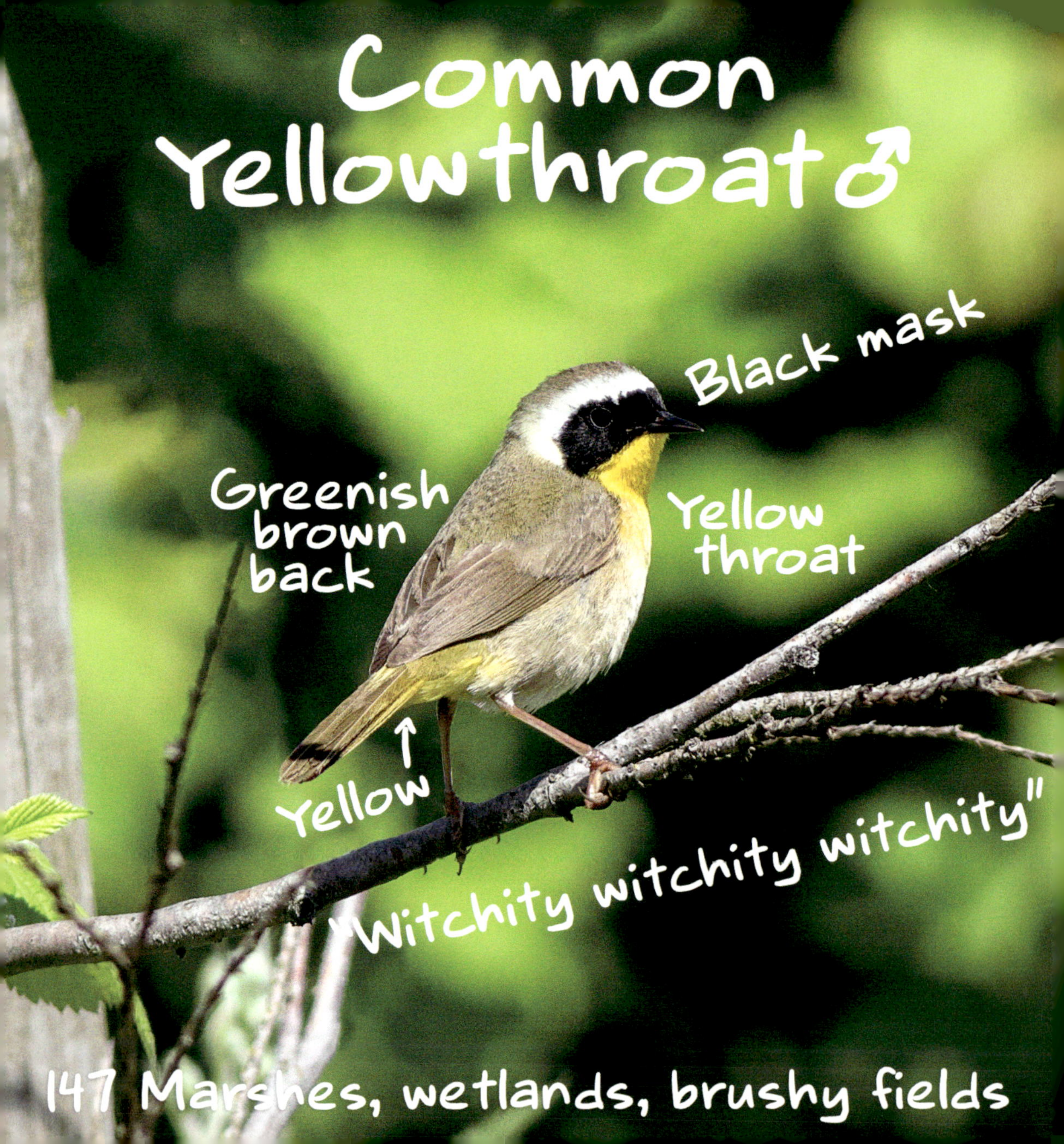

Common Yellowthroat ♂

Black mask

Greenish brown back

Yellow throat

↑ Yellow

"Witchity witchity witchity"

 Marshes, wetlands, brushy fields

Common Yellowthroat ♀

Brown face & back

Yellow throat

Yellow undertail

Hides in tall grass

Yellow-rumped Warbler
(Audubon's subspecies)

"Chep"

Yellow throat

Yellow sides

Black streaking

Our year-round warbler

Yellow-rumped Warbler

(Myrtle subspecies)

"Chep"

Black cheek

Yellow patch

White throat

Streaked chest

"Chep"

Eats berries & suet in fall/winter

Yellow-rumped Warbler (first winter)

White eye arcs

Brownish top

Pale throat

Light streaks

Subtle yellow sides

"Chep"

Winter resident, eats suet

Yellow-rumped Warbler (adult breeding)

"Chep"

Yellow spot

Blue-gray back

White wing coverts

All have Yellow rumps!

Often heard chipping & seen flycatching

"Chep"

Nicknamed "butter butt"

Townsend's Warbler

 Conifer-loving winter warbler

Black-throated Gray Warbler

Winters in Mexico
breeds here May-Sep

Western Tanager ♂

frog-like "pridit"

Red face

Black back

Yellow rump

Hunts bugs & berries in upper canopy

Western Tanager ♀
Yellowish head
Grayish back
Chunky bill
Wing bars
Dark tail & wings

Black-headed Grosbeak ♂

Black head

Enormous bill

Sounds like a melodic robin

Orange chest

Black & white wings

Yellow sprinkles

Black-headed Grosbeak

(female/immature)

Stripy face

Call: "Zwick"

Streaked back

Big bill

Orange

Feeder bird later in breeding season

Photo Credits

For a digital list and links to photographers' Creative Commons photos visit: pdxbirder.com/cc All photos edited by Eric R. Carlson.

Andy Reago & Chrissy McClarren - CC BY 2.0
54 Cooper's Hawk
69 Red-shouldered Hawk
75 Barn Owl
83 Acorn Woodpecker
110 Swainson's Thrush

Bering Land Bridge National Preserve CC BY 2.0
14 Green-Winged Teal Duck

Bettina Arrigoni - CC BY 2.0
143 Olive-sided Flycatcher | Sabine Woods | High Island | TX|2018-04-26|09-14-16.jpg

Bill Thomson - CC BY 2.0
41 Purple Martin

Colby Stopa - CC BY 2.0
156 Western Tanager-Piranga ludoviciana

Denis Fournier - CC BY 2.0
35 Bihoreau gris - Black-crowned Night Heron

Laura Wolf - CC BY 2.0
114 house sparrow cromwell valley 6.16.20 DSC_0265
137 edit brown-headed cowbird neighborhood 4.2.20 DSC_0245

Becky Matsubara - CC BY 2.0
13 Green-winged Teal (m)
20 Bufflehead (f)
46 Cliff Swallow
58 Sharp-shinned Hawk (juvenile)
70 Red-shouldered Hawk
73 Great-horned Owl
78 Peregrine Falcon (juvenile)
80 Hairy Woodpecker
93 Oak Titmouse with sunflower seed
102 Bewick's Wren
105 Band-tailed Pigeon
106 Eurasian Collared-Dove
141 European Starling
153 Townsend's Warbler (m)
157 Black-headed Grosbeak (m)

David St. Louis - CC BY 2.0
77 Merlin 2

Ik T - CC BY 2.0
12 オナガガモ ー 本埜「白鳥の郷」

John Benson - CC BY 2.0
43 Tree Swallow

Larry Lamsa - CC BY 2.0
49 Rufous Hummingbird
50 Female Rufous Hummingbird
123 Pine Siskin

Joachim Bertrands - All rights reserved
40 Vaux's Swift

Russ Whitehurst - CC BY 2.0
36 immature black-crowned night heron alighting, gamecock cottage
56 sharp-shinned hawk on wing ventral

Ryan Mandelbaum - CC BY 2.0
71 red-shouldered hawk - brooklyn, ny

Shenandoah National Park (public domain)
98 White-breasted Nuthatch
117 Purple Finch (male)
118 Purple Finch (female)
121 American Goldfinch
122 American Goldfinch

Marneejill CC BY-SA 2.0
38 female belted kingfisher

Sunny - CC BY 2.0
57 Sharp Shinned Hawk Sun bathing

USFWS Midwest Region (public domain)
31 Spotted sandpiper

USFWS Mountain-Prairie (public domain)
6 Northern shoveler at Seedskadee National Wildlife Refuge
8 Gadwall Hen on Seedskadee National Wildlife Refuge
11 Northern pintail at Seedskadee National Wildlife Refuge
26 Ruddy duck at Seedskadee National Wildlife Refuge
61 Golden eagle in Wyoming
62 Golden eagle on Seedskadee National Wildlife Refuge
66 Red-Tailed Hawk Rufous Morph Adult Seedskadee NWR
103 Marsh wren at Seedskadee National Wildlife Refuge

All other photos by Eric R. Carlson - All rights reserved

An ENORMOUS thank-you to everyone on the internet who opts in to allow their photos to be used by others. This book would not have been possible without those of you generous enough to tag your photos with Creative Commons licenses.

Blackbird,
Brewer's 139-140
Red-winged 135-136
Bluebird, Western 108
Bufflehead 19-20
Bushtit 99
Chickadee,
Black-capped 91
Chestnut-backed 92
Collared-Dove,
Eurasian 106
Coot, American 28
Cormorant, Double-crested 37
Cowbird, Brown-headed 137-138
Creeper, Brown 100
Crow, American 87-88
Dove, Mourning 107
Duck,
Ring-necked 15-16
Ruddy 25-26
Wood 17-18
Eagle,
Bald 59-60
Golden 61-62
Egret, Great 34
Falcon, Peregrine 78
Finch,
House 115-116
Purple 117 - 118
Flicker, Northern 81
Flycatcher,
Olive-sided 143
Gadwall 7-8
Goldfinch,
American 121-122
Lesser 119-120
Goose,
Cackling 1
Canada 2
Grebe, Pied-billed 27
Grosbeak,
Black-headed 157-158
Hawk,
Cooper's 53-55
Red-shouldered 69-71
Red-tailed 63-68
Sharp-shinned 56-58
Heron,
Black-crowned Night 35-36
Great Blue 33
Hummingbird
Anna's 47-48
Rufous 49-50
Jay,
California Scrub 86
Steller's 85
Junco, Dark-eyed 124
Kestrel, American 76
Killdeer 29
Kingfisher, Belted 38
Kinglet,
Golden-crowned 94
Ruby-crowned 95
Kite, White-tailed 72
Mallard 3-4
Martin, Purple 41-42
Merganser,
Common 23-24
Hooded 21-22
Merlin 77
Nuthatch,
Red-breasted 97
White-breasted 98
Osprey 52
Owl,
Barn 75
Barred 74
Great Horned 73
Phoebe, Black 39
Pigeon,
Band-tailed 105
Rock 104
Pintail, Northern 11-12
Raven, Common 89-90
Robin, American 112
Sandpiper,
Spotted 31-32
Sapsucker,
Red-breasted 82
Shoveler, Northern 5-6
Siskin, Pine 123
Sparrow,
Fox 126
Golden-crowned129-130
House 113-114
Lincoln's 134
Savannah 133
Song 125
White-crowned 127-128
White-throated 131
Starling, European 141
Swallow,
Barn 45
Cliff 46
Tree 43
Violet-green 44
Swift, Vaux's 40
Tanager,
Western 155-156
Teal,
Green-winged 13-14
Thrush,
Hermit 109
Swainson's 110
Varied 111
Titmouse, Oak 93
Towhee, Spotted 132
Vireo,
Hutton's 96
Warbling 144
Vulture, Turkey 51
Warbler,
Black-throated Gray 154
Orange-crowned 145
Townsend's 153
Wilson's 146
Yellow-rumped 149-152
Waxwing, Cedar 142
Wigeon, American 9
Woodpecker,
Acorn 83
Downy 79
Hairy 80
Pileated 84
Wren,
Bewick's 102
Marsh 103
Pacific 101
Yellowlegs, Greater 30
Yellowthroat, Common 147-148